BACKYARD SAFARI

Deer

Wil Mara

Cavendish
Square

New York

Published in 2014 by Cavendish Square Publishing, LLC
303 Park Avenue South, Suite 1247, New York, NY 10010

Website: cavendishsq.com

This publication represents the opinions and views of the author based on his or her personal experience, knowledge, and research. The information in this book serves as a general guide only. The author and publisher have used their best efforts in preparing this book and disclaim liability rising directly or indirectly from the use and application of this book.

CPSIA Compliance Information. Batch #WW14CSQ

All websites were available and accurate when this book was sent to press.

Library of Congress Cataloging-in-Publication Data

Mara, Wil.
Deer / by Wil Mara.
p. cm. — (Backyard safari)
Includes index.
ISBN 978-1-62712-304-4 (hardcover) ISBN 978-1-62712-305-1 (paperback) ISBN 978-1-62712-306-8 (e-book)
1. Deer — Juvenile literature. I. Mara, Wil. II. Title.
QL737.U55 M28 2014
599.65—dc23

Editorial Director: Dean Miller
Senior Editor: Peter Mavrikis
Copy Editor: Cynthia Roby
Art Director: Jeffrey Talbot
Designer: Joseph Macri
Photo Researcher: Alison Morretta
Production Manager: Jennifer Ryder-Talbot
Production Editor: Andrew Coddington

The photographs in this book are used by permission and through the courtesy of: Cover photo by Don Johnston/All Canada Photos/Getty Images; Biosphoto / SuperStock, 4; John Cancalosi/Peter Arnold/Getty Images, 6; Animals Animals / SuperStock, 8; David Lyons / age fotostock / SuperStock, 9; Terry A Parker/All Canada Photos/Getty Images, 10; Steve Bloom Images / SuperStock, 11; Wayne Lynch / All Canada Photos / SuperStock, 12; ClassicStock.com / SuperStock, 13; John Serrao/Photo Researchers/Getty Images, 15; Photos by Michael Crowley/Flickr, Getty Images, 16; Linda Freshwaters Arndt/Photo Researchers/Getty Images, 17; age fotostock / SuperStock. 18; Danita Delimont/Gallo Images, 20; age fotostock / SuperStock, 21; age fotostock / SuperStock, 23; Larry Landolfi/Photo Researchers/Getty Images, 24; Don White / SuperStock, 24; Sven-Erik Arndt/Picture Press/Getty Images, 24; Dickson Images/ Photolibrary/Getty Images, 24; imagebroker.net / SuperStock, 26; Gary K Smith/Garden Picture Library/Getty Images, 27; Jeff Greenberg/Photolibrary/ Getty Images, 28.

Printed in the United States of America

Contents

Introduction

Have you ever watched a squirrel chasing another squirrel around a tree? Or a group of deer leaping gracefully through a stretch of winter woods? If you have, then you know how wonderful it is to discover nature for yourself. Each book in the Backyard Safari series takes you step-by-step on an easy outdoor adventure, and then helps you identify the animals you've found. You'll also learn ways to attract, observe, and protect these valuable creatures. As you read, be on the lookout for the Safari Tips and Trek Talk facts sprinkled throughout the book. Ready? The fun starts just steps from your back door!

ONE
A Deer's Life

Deer Bodies

Deer are members of a class of animal known as **mammals** (which includes you too, by the way). They are also in an animal family called **Cervidae**. Deer have been around a long time, with fossils in Europe dating back as far as 30 million years. They generally range in weight from around 75 pounds (34 kg) to as much as ten times that (750 lbs / 340 kg). A few adult deer have been known to weigh as little as 20 pounds (9 kg) and as much as 1,000 pounds (453.5 kg) or even a bit more. There's a lot of variety! Deer are four-legged animals with sleek oval bodies, short tails, longish necks, and large ears. A deer's legs may appear spindly and somewhat "weak" in comparison to the rest of their bodies. But make no mistake—they are very powerful, enabling a deer to travel at great speeds and leap over tall obstacles. Their hooves have a split toe and are tough enough to withstand even the most difficult terrain.

In terms of coloration, fur on most adult deer **species** is some shade of brown—light, dark, reddish, or yellowish. A few species are white

Most deer species are brown in color, with dark eyes and white undersides.

while others are gray. Many deer have whitish undersides—the belly, under the neck and chin, inside the legs—and very often a whitish ring around their very dark (often black) noses. Their eyes are round and dark and are also sometimes ringed in white. Newborns appear quite different from the adults. They will have a peppering of spots along the sides, which will fade as they grow into adulthood.

The males of most species grow **antlers**, or branch-like horns, from the top of their head once they reach a certain age. Females can also sprout little stubs, but these are nowhere near as prominent as the males' antlers (female reindeer, however, do grow full-size antlers that are every bit as impressive as those of their male counterparts). Antlers are used for the mating season, mostly to fight off other males. At the end of the mating season, they will fall off.

Trek Talk

There is a fairly rare variety of deer coloration known as **piebald**, in which a deer has a distinctly patchy design of very light (sometimes even white) colors along with its normal browns or grays. Such deer almost look as if they were being painted and the painter left them "unfinished." While they are a fascinating sight to see, piebald deer are particularly susceptible to **predators** because they can't hide as easily among the dark colors of the forest.

Deer with "piebald" coloration—large areas of white (or, more precisely, a lack of color)—are quite rare.

Where They Live

Deer species can be found on every continent except Antarctica and Australia. Africa has the fewest deer species—just one, found in the northeastern area—whereas Asia has the most. There are deer in many different **environments**, from cold regions of the extreme north, and south to some of the warmest areas of the tropics. They can be found in a wide variety of **habitats**—everything from deserts and swamps to mountains and grassy plains—but most prefer wooded areas with plenty of overgrowth for cover. Deer are timid by nature, and they must have adequate places to hide in order to feel comfortable. They try to avoid contact with humans and certainly do not want interaction with predators, of which they have many. They will venture into the open during the day in order to feed and to get around. It is not unusual to see them in heavily populated areas, including some cities. If deer do not sense danger, they will **graze** almost anywhere there are feeding opportunities, including sports fields, public parks, and people's front or back yards.

Deer are not generally solitary animals—they are usually seen in groups.

What They Do

Deer can be active day or night. Most species are active during the day, particularly during dawn and dusk (sunrise and sunset). They spend much of their waking hours foraging for food. They are **herbivorous**, which means they only eat plants. A hungry deer will consume everything from fruits, vegetables, and nuts to a variety of grasses, leafy plants, flowers, twigs and branches, and even tree bark. In colder climates, deer will eat less food in the winter simply because there isn't as much available. This also means the deer will be less active because they won't have as much energy to burn. Deer do not hibernate in the winter like many other mammals. They are able to withstand the cold due to the thickness of their hides. They will, however, sleep longer hours to use less energy. Even in winter, they are susceptible to predators. Some of the most common animals that hunt

Deer can be active both day and night.

deer include large cats such as cougars and mountain lions, wolves and coyotes, bears, alligators and crocodiles, and, of course, human beings. Since deer are such popular **prey**, they have evolved into alert and nervous animals. This is one of the reasons they travel in **herds**.

The Cycle of Life

The time of year deer breed depends on where they live and their species. For most deer, the mating season occurs in the late summer or fall. The young, known as **fawns**, are born in spring or early summer. The **gestation** period for a female, meaning the time it takes for the fawn to develop, can run anywhere from seven to ten months. The mother will usually give birth (to just one fawn) away from the rest of the herd. She will pick an area with heavy vegetation to provide maximum cover. Once the fawn is born,

As the saying goes: "There is safety in numbers."

the mother will lick it clean so it will not give off a scent to predators. The mother will then try to nudge the fawn to stand up, which it can usually do within its first half hour! The fawn will remain hidden for the first month or so to protect it from predators. It will then join the rest of the herd and remain in the protective presence of its mother for about a year. Then the mother will encourage it to move off on its own in order to make room for the next fawn. Most deer live about 10 to 15 years in the wild.

Young deer usually have spots on their bodies, which will fade over time.

TWO

You Are the Explorer

Just because deer are timid and watchful, don't think you won't be able to see a few! The number-one rule on a deer safari is to remember that you should never try to get too close. If you keep a reasonable distance away, you should be able to enjoy the sight of these magnificent animals for quite awhile. Also remember that deer herds that live in an area heavily populated by people are used to seeing people around. That means they'll relax and "do their thing" as long as you don't do anything to frighten them off.

These campers have picked a perfect moment to look outside their tent!

What Do I Wear?

✳ Old clothes that can get dirty.

✳ Clothes that are loose-fitting and, most importantly, comfortable.

✳ Clothes that are dull in color (black, brown, or gray). If you wear brightly colored clothes—clothes of a color that is not normally seen in the wild—you could definitely scare off a deer.

✳ Any type of shoes will do, but those with soft soles are best. These will be the quietest, and the less noise you make the better.

✳ Bug spray

What Do I Take?

✳ Binoculars. This will be your most valuable tool when it comes to observing deer on your safari.

✳ Digital camera, preferably one with good zoom capabilities.

✳ Notebook

✳ Cell phone

✳ Pen or pencil

✳ Folding chair

✳ A snack for yourself

Where Do I Go?

Fortunately for you, deer can be found just about anywhere. They prefer the secrecy of thick woodlands, but they do venture into the open from time to time. They also tend not to sit around much and are frequently on the move. That means you've got a fairly good chance of coming across a few. And since they travel in groups, you're likely to see more than one at a time.

❋ Forested areas. Deer prefer to remain among the protective cover of trees and shrubs and other shaded places. If you live near a forest, then you've got a fairly good chance of seeing a few.

You'll need a lot of patience and a willingness to keep very quiet in order to spot a deer in the wild. They're always on the lookout for danger.

* Fields with plenty of overgrowth. Think about what deer like to eat: plants, plants, and more plants! Go to places where you'll find these things. Deer will venture into open fields, along grassy margins, around the edges of farms, and anyplace else that offers feeding opportunities. Look around and try to think like a deer—you'll be amazed at what you'll find.

* Gardens and flower beds. If you live in an area where deer are common and you have neighbors who take great pride in their landscaping, then you've probably heard those same neighbors complain that the local deer will come into their yard and eat their fruits, vegetables, or flowers.

* Farmlands. Farms are often a good place to spot deer, especially along the edges and the far-back areas. There's usually plenty of food for them plus several places to hide. Deer love to walk through tall rows of corn, for example, because they will be hard to see and there's a lot to eat!

This young deer has relatively small but very obvious antler growth.

Deer can often be seen by bodies of water since they need to drink like most other animals.

❋ Near water. Deer have to drink just like other wild animals, and they frequently do so from streams, rivers, lakes, and ponds. This isn't to say they'll spend all their time along quiet shorelines, but areas with a reliable water source will attract their attention.

It's very important to remember that you should always be with an adult that you trust when you go on your deer safari. It can be very risky to walk around alone. Also, if you go on someone else's property, make sure you have permission to do so. You can get into a lot of trouble for trespassing.

What Do I Do?

❇ Watch for movement. The best approach for you to take is to find a comfortable spot for yourself, then scan your surroundings in search of movement.

❇ Go out at the right time. Deer can be out and about most any time of day, but the best is in the early morning (around sunrise) or in the evening (sunset). This is when they feel safest and will come out to feed.

❇ Listen. You shouldn't make too much noise when you go on your safari—but deer often do. Although they often take very gentle steps, if something frightens them they'll take off running and crash through just about everything in front them. When this happens, you've got a great opportunity to spot them.

If a deer realizes you're watching it, you need to remain very still. If you make any sudden movements, it won't stick around for long.

* Keep still and quiet. Deer can be surprisingly tolerant of people—as long as we don't get too close or make too much noise.

* Hide yourself. Want to make your deer safari really interesting? Find a hiding spot out there in the wild, someplace where the deer won't easily be able to see you, such as a big shrub or on the ground behind some large rocks.

Safari Tip

If you have the opportunity to watch deer from the comfort of a car, do so! Deer generally do not recognize cars as a danger and will often walk right past them (as long as they're parked with the motor off, of course). If you keep your camera handy and remain reasonably still, you can get some amazingly good pictures.

Moose are related to deer and are very common in some parts of North America. But beware—they are much more powerful and can be very temperamental.

❋ Be patient. Don't expect to find a giant herd of deer the moment you walk out your door. In fact, don't be surprised if you don't see any deer during your first few safaris. Remember that deer live in the wild all the time and are experts at sensing danger. This means they might know you're there long before you know they're there.

❋ Keep your camera ready. It's not too hard to take a few nice pictures of deer once you've spotted them, but you need to be ready for such opportunities. Don't leave the camera off thinking you'll have plenty of time when deer come along. Since they're so skittish, or easily frightened, you never know when they're going to take off running. Also, try to avoid using a flash if you can help it.

❋ Keep notes. When you finally do see a few deer, write down any information in your notebook that you feel is important. What did they look like? How big were they? Where were you when you saw them? What time of day did you see them? After you gather enough data, you'll begin to recognize patterns that'll help you with future safaris.

❋ Back home, download any pictures or videos you took. Show them to your friends and family. You could also write a formal journal using both your pictures and your notes. Keep an ongoing record of your deer safaris from year to year.

Make sure you keep detailed notes of your deer observations—they will be helpful on future safaris.

THREE
A Guide to Deer

There are only a few deer species in North America. This should make it fairly easy for you to identify those that you find during your safari. The two most common and widespread, by far, are the White-tailed deer (Odocoileus virginianus) and the Mule deer (Odocoileus hemionus). But there are a few others, and you should know how to tell them apart. Start by going over the points given below.

* Look over the notes you took while you were "in the field." Now, try to answer the following questions:

* What was the deer's basic appearance? What was its "base" color?

* Aside from its base color, did it have any other coloration? What about on its belly or the underside of its neck? And what about around the tail?

* Were there any other distinct markings? Rings around the nose or the eyes?

* Were there any fawns in the herd that you saw? If so, how did they look (coloration or spotting)?

✱ Did it have antlers? If so, how would you describe them?

✱ What did the tail look like? Was it thin and ropey, or was it more like a little flame shape? Did it hang down and wave around, or did it stick up in the air?

Deer antlers can grow quite large and look similar to the branches of a dead tree.

Now, go to the next page and see if any of the deer in the photos match up with the **characteristics** that you noted in your answers. And remember that you should use other information such as your location (town, state, country) and the exact habitat in which you saw them to provide the final pieces of your puzzle. Try doing a little research on the Internet, too. Further resources are also provided for you in this book's Find Out More section.

White-tailed Deer

Black-tailed Deer

Red Deer

Mule Deer

FOUR

Try This! Projects You Can Do

Deer might be a little too nervous, not to mention a little too big, for you to keep as pets. But there are still plenty of hands-on things you can do to further your enjoyment of studying them.

Making Tracks

One of the most exciting sights for any safari enthusiast is finding deer tracks along the ground. They will appear like a pair of long teardrops next to each other, but not quite touching. These tracks usually disappear within a very short period of time, from rain, wind, trampling by other animals, and so on. But if you do find some nice-looking tracks, there is a fun and easy way for you to "capture" them forever. Bring along three buckets—one with plaster of Paris (available at most craft stores), another with water, and an empty one. Mix the plaster of Paris and the water in the empty bucket until you have a batter that is thick enough so that it isn't watery or runny, but still thin enough to pour.

Then, carefully pour it into one of the **hoof** prints. Leave it there for about an hour so it will dry into a mold. Then lift the mold out of the track. When you get home, gently press the mold into some soft clay. Once the clay hardens, you will have a perfect replica of a real deer track.

One sure sign that you're in deer territory is a set of deer tracks.

Feeding Time

You won't be able to feed a deer in your house as you would a normal pet, but you can still feed them in the wild. If you have deer close to your home you can leave food out for them, but make sure you stay out of sight. Remember that deer are opportunistic feeders, which means they'll eat pretty much whatever they come across. If you set out some cut-up vegetables such as carrots or corn, fruits such as apples and oranges, oats or barley, or even a few salt blocks, there's a good chance your local deer will discover them and have a nice meal. Some deer-watchers like to leave a "trail" of these items that leads up to their homes. As long as you don't go outside and scare the deer, this is a good way to get a very close look at them. If you stay near a window with your camera ready, you'll get some incredibly good photos.

Deer will be drawn to a wide variety of vegetables.

Deer Emergency

During one of your safaris, you might encounter a deer that is either sick or wounded. Sad to say, many people hunt them, and sometimes they only wound them. In such cases, you may be tempted to get close to the deer in attempt to help it. Don't. If you have an adult with you (which you should), ask that person to call your local animal control organization, zoo, or police department. A deer that is sick or hurt will already be frightened. The sight of a human coming close will cause it to become even more scared, and the animal may react violently or hurt itself further. Even though deer are herbivorous, they are also very powerful and can harm you. Also remember that deer are known to carry ticks that can cause diseases in humans. So if you see one that is suffering, be smart and get help—don't try to handle the situation yourself.

Glossary

antlers   branch-like horns that grow from the top of a deer's (usually male) head

Cervidae   a class of animals that includes all deer

characteristic   a specific trait or quality that an animal has, such as tan fur or brown eyes

environment   where an animal lives, such as a forest, swamp, or desert

fawn   a newborn or very young deer

gestation   amount of time it takes a baby to develop inside its mother

graze   to feed on, or eat, grasses

habitat   the exact type of place in which an animal lives, such as a burrow, cave, or shoreline

herbivorous   only eating plants

herd   a group of animals of the same species

hoof   a deer's foot

mammal   any animal belonging to the class known as Mammalia

piebald   coloration with a very light base (often white) covered with irregular dark patches

predator   an animal that hunts other animals

prey   any animal that is hunted by another animal

species   one particular type of animal

Find Out More

Books

Magby, Meryl. *White-tailed Deer*. New York: PowerKids Press, 2013.

Riggs, Kate. *Moose*. New York: PowerKids Press, 2012.

Webster, Christine. *Deer with Code*. New York: Weigl, 2012.

Websites

White-tailed Deer for Kids / National Geographic

animals.nationalgeographic.com/animals/mammals/white-tailed-deer/

Fun and colorful information page about White-tailed Deer—one of the most common species in North America—on the National Geographic website. Includes pictures and audio clips, fast facts, maps, and more!

Fun Deer Facts for Kids / Science Kids

sciencekids.co.nz/sciencefacts/animals/deer.html

A great list of unusual and interesting facts about deer presented by the popular "Science Kids" site.

Mule Deer / San Diego Zoo

kids.sandiegozoo.org/animals/mammals/mule-deer

Lots of basic information about the Mule Deer, another common North American species, on the kids' site from the San Diego Zoo. Plus photos, facts, audio, and more!